Mini Habits

The Little Things That Change Everything

Logan Williamson

Table of Contents

Introduction

Habits, over a period of time, become part of us due to constant activity or a series of constant activities. We are faced daily with decisions that have the potential to affect our lives and the lives of the people around us. Little do most of us know that our habits, whether good or bad, is the fuel with which our life runs.

It is important for emotional and mental maturity. It is also helpful in achieving your set goals. Resilience and willpower are some of the necessary factors for strong habit formation. The importance of good habits cannot be overemphasized, and the importance of building our already established good habits can also not be overstated.

This book gives an in-depth knowledge of how mini-habits lead to even more life-changing habits, and how they (positive life-changing habits) can be achieved in no time. This book looks at the importance of willpower as compared to motivation in building one's habit and also takes a look at the detractors of good habits.

The intention is that at the end of reading this book, you will be better equipped to start and stick with healthy habits. The road to success may not be quite easy, but it definitely is not as hard as you think.

Start building your foundation for a life of happiness and success in all aspects of your life. Start working on building your habits

Chapter 1: The Concept of Habits

"We are what we repeatedly do. Excellence, then, is not an act, but a habit."

~ Aristotle

Understanding Habits

Every day, we perform dozens of activities. Some of them are so mundane that we barely even remember them. Like, who really keeps track of how many times they turn handles to open doors, or the mechanical way we get to places we know well?

These overlooked activities, which seem to take almost no intention to carry out, are called habits. Habit can be traced to the Latin word *habitare,* which means "to live," and they certainly do affect how we live.

The Oxford Dictionary defines a habit as, "A thing that you do often and almost without thinking, especially something that is hard to stop doing."

From nervously tapping your feet, being particular about putting on both socks before shoes, to eating or sleeping at a certain time, if you were to ask the average person why they do any (or all) of this, the answers you can expect will go like this: "I'm not really sure," "I didn't even know I did that," or "Guess I'm just used to it." So, it can be inferred that most habitual activities stem from the subconscious, where they require little directive from the brain and are usually hard to desist from. But just how deeply rooted are these behaviors?

Exploring the Psychology of Habits

The brain, as the primary center of direction, is the main determinant in habit formation. Psychologists have long since strived to make sense of the things we do, and why we do them. From its advent, their research has examined our physical make-up, emotional states, and reactions to various situations in order to understand just what makes humans tick. This quest led to the birth of many different schools of thought and theories, ranging from Wundt's premiere Structuralism to Freud's popular Psychoanalysis. As far as understanding habits goes though, Behaviorism, which focuses on observable actions, seems most comprehensive for our study and is widely applied in therapy today.

Under this theory, Russian psychologist, Ivan Pavlov developed the system of conditioning. This has to do with the process of cultivating and acclimatizing humans and animals to certain patterns of action.

The eminent practitioners John B. Watson and B.F. Skinner made further instrumental finds in Conditioning.

Watson, in his Classical Theory, stressed the role that association plays in forming behavioral patterns. For him, habits were built through the mind tying a natural response to a certain type of stimuli, leading to the inherent assumption that where there was one, the other was sure to follow. This impression on the brain would be so strong, that even when the stimuli were not there, the assumption remained.

To sum this up, we might consider someone used to passing a particular obstacle on the path to their location, a type of barricade, for example. Following a period long enough for them to become accustomed to the blockade, if you were to eventually remove it, you'd notice that at least for a short while after, the person would continue to dodge this invisible object on autopilot.

Skinner, however, focused on the roles punishment and reward played on behavior in his Operant Theory. He opined that the consequences, whether positive or negative, one must face after doing something would determine their interest in repeating it. This method has become popular in teaching children. When a behavior produces an enjoyable effect, it makes the brain release a chemical called *dopamine* (a neurotransmitter dealing in focus), which creates a craving for more. There are gratifying ways to achieve this, like exercise and achieving a goal, and inadvisable ones, like eating junk food or binge shopping.

The Fidget

There is a range of habits to consider, besides the most discussed: eating, sleeping, drinking, etc. The ones more evident, and often quite annoying to those around, however, are nervous habits.

People usually develop nervous habits as a way to self-soothe in uncertain or alarming situations. They usually involve some sort of rhythmic activity in which the brain tries to fulfill a need to alter the environment on the inside.

These coping mechanisms include thumb-sucking, leg shaking, picking skin, finger tapping, fussing, pencil/pen biting, playing with hair or ear touching, bruxism, eye-contact avoidance, vocal tics, and nail-biting.

If you find yourself stuck with some of these behaviors, you may have found been victim to the generic, "That's a dirty habit!" Actually, a number of them could end up harming you.

Thumb, or any other finger, sucking could lead to a transfer of bacteria from the skin to the mouth (or the other way round) and subsequent infections. Nail-biting, aside from being unpleasant to look at, results in the ingestion of germs under the fingernails, which could bring stomach upsets. Bruxism (clenching and grinding of teeth) ends in tooth cracking or jaw problems. Licking or biting the lips makes the enzymes in saliva dry the lips until they crack, and get a burning sensation. Chewing writing implements may land you swallowing any type of virus that might be on them. Playing with the hair, especially if it's a particular segment, could result in bald spots. And lastly, pimple popping might get you permanent scars or even worse if you affect a blood vessel or nerve, by accident.

Ultimately, it is in anyone's best interest to try and trump their regular nervous habits (keeping in mind that real obsessive behavior requires professional intervention).

Getting Stuck in One's Ways

We now have a fuller comprehension of just what habits are, but are yet to grasp *why* we have them.

This has to do with the brain as a control center. According to assistant professor of psychology, Christina Gremel in a study undertaken by the University of California, circuits that direct habitual actions and those for goal-oriented behavior vie for dominance in the part of the brain responsible for decision-making, the basal ganglia. The brain has a habit of storing processes we ritually undergo, a bit like a cache in computing. It does this to increase efficacy, ensuring speed in performing routine activities, without too much thought. Imagine having to relearn how to climb stairs or brush your teeth each time.

So, habits are there to make daily cycles run smoothly. The problem, however, is that a good number of these acquired behaviors are unproductive.

Out with the Old, In with the New

People are naturally creatures of habit and tend to avoid going out of their way to do things that are viewed as stressful or do not instantaneously yield satisfaction. What this means is, change is hard.

This seems to be especially true of getting into more positive routines. Many of us can't seem to forgo having that extra sugary treat or skipping the exercise slot we promised to stick to. Luckily, as a learned behavior, habits can also be unlearned!

Made up of three elements, habits are absorbed in a cycle: cue, response, and reward. What this means is that, in order to create or eliminate a habit, we need to identify what elicits a type of behavior/emotion, monitor our reactions and the result thereafter.

Cue: The situation, location, emotion, people, whatever. It is necessary you do some introspective, and figure out just what it is that triggers your negative habit. Like, if you find yourself tempted to overeat during the holidays, or bite your nails during tests, it remains to discover the impulse behind this, be it, over-stimulation, boredom, or lethargy.

Response: Once you can say for sure what it is that pushes you down a certain route, it is time to actively do something contrary. A person who is prone to anxiety when faced with deadlines, who recognizes that this is caused by the fear of not being able to deliver on time, needs to, when it arises, determine to encourage themselves and draw up a plan for time-management.

Reward: Always keeping in mind the goal or long-term reward is important, but it is equally useful to remember to give oneself intermittent treats and celebrate even the smallest victories.

Swap!

Habits of any sort are the brain's retort to some kind of stimuli. Putting in the effort to simply get rid of a habit is somewhat risky because it means there is a need being left unmet. "Just stop doing it" is never the right answer, not only because it is overly simplistic (even inconsiderate), but also, because things simply don't work that way.

As it happens, habits are easier to replace than completely eliminate; and the fact is, if the cue is left unattended to, the bad habit is likely to return or be subconsciously replaced with something similar. You might have seen people assuming they were on successful diets because they deprived themselves of food, but picked up a drinking problem or were in perpetually bad spirits.

The Need for Change

So far, from all that's been written to this point, it seems like creating meaningful changes in our lives requires a bit of work. What's really in it for all that effort?

The answer is balance and improvement in any of the essential areas of our lives:

- **Health**: adopting better eating, sleeping, exercise habits or determining to have more frequent checkups.
    - Benefits: maintaining a healthy weight, more efficacious organs, lifted mood, being able to catch diseases early.
- **Family and friends**: spending more time with loved ones.
    - Benefits: improved relationships, and a more grounded support system.
- **Self-care:** giving attention to things that bring you pleasure, hobbies, or alone time.
    - Benefits: feeling less taken advantage of and more accomplished, sustaining a sense of individuality.
- **Emotional health**: cutting off or restricting exposure to practices or people who tend to drain you.
    - Benefits: less animosity towards these triggers.
- **Love life**: making time for, or better decisions in intimate relationships.
    - Benefits: closer affiliation and stronger bond.
- **Stress decadence**: curbing over-indulgence in junk food, TV marathons, and alcohol as ways to let off steam.
    - Benefits: decrease in guilt, self-flagellation; health benefits.
- **Personality growth**: identifying and making amends to personal flaws.
    - Benefits: a sense of evolution, pride.
- **Career or business**: being more efficient at work.
    - Benefits: achieving more, opportunity for recognition, less burn-out.
- **Finance management**: cultivating better spending/saving habits.
    - Benefits: ebbing anxiety about the future, ability to fund hobbies or emergencies.
- **Community contribution**: giving back to those around.
    - Benefits: strengthening associations, gratification.

- **Environmental care**: being less messy, making environmentally friendly choices.
  - Benefits: less guilt/self-flagellation, satisfaction, pride, comfortable habitation, ease, a greater good.

Success in these vital aspects leads to increased energy, confidence, and more ambition

No Time Like the Present!

If you've found yourself making New Year's resolutions after New Year's resolutions to stick to a diet and finally lose some weight or instill some new personality trait, but are yet to succeed, you may simply be going about it all wrong. It is certainly doable with the right techniques and a positive outlook.

Habits are like saved pages in a browser: there to give you easier access. But, some of these pages have become unnecessary, or may even be harmful long-term. Newly found knowledge that by willful action (which becomes a fresh habit) we can re-order our behavior is life-changing information, but can only be helpful if applied. This New Year, make your life run smoother by clearing out unconstructive habits...and possibly some of the actual browser tabs, while we're at it.

Chapter 2: Myths About Habits

"The soul, like the body, accepts by practice whatever habit one wishes it to contact."

~ Socrates

1. Hearsay: Every topic under the sun has some myths attached to it – habits are no different. Lack of accurate information in the past, unfounded evidence (what is known as "junk science"), and a well of assumptions led to many incorrect ideas about how habits work, how new ones are formed, and how long it takes for them to become a solid part of your routine.

If we are going to actually restructure our habits this time around, it will be necessary to delve into and debunk some of this fiction.

2. 3 weeks tops: One of the most common myths about habit formation is that it takes place within a set time of about 21 days. This most likely springs from the impression given by the leading self-help book from the 1960s *Psycho Cybernetic*. According to the author, Maxwell Maltz, "It usually requires a minimum of about 21 days to effect any perceptible change in a mental image," and this assumption has stuck until recent times.

Truth be told (in alignment with more recent studies), it actually takes anywhere from 18 days to almost a year. The average, however, seems to be 66 days, depending on the person and habit in question.

3. The will to carry on: Another very common assumption is that you need to have a will of steel to get into a new routine. You hear so many people talking about how their failed efforts are down to being "mentally weak" or "not having wanted it hard enough." Having understood how habits work to the extent we have, it becomes clear how untrue this is. Far more productive is routinely performing the task, until it becomes a part of you.

4. Over and over: In reference to the best ways to establish habits, something you are bound to hear about is repetition. Not to imply that this is totally wrong; we do know a habit to be an act that has become automatic due to the frequency it is performed, after all. The thing is, when it comes to habits you are trying to deliberately learn, it is more effective to do them routinely and on cue (at scheduled intervals, locations or instances), than simply repeating the behavior. A reasonable illustration of this would be somebody attempting to exercise more. It would hardly make sense to direct them to start doing squats at random while in the kitchen, and such a practice would probably lead faster to them abandoning this resolution than building it into a habit.

5. 365: In stressing the importance of sticking to a new regime, it is said that every day matters and consistency is of the utmost importance. A person who wanted to go vegetarian cracks and eats a ham sandwich on Day 17, and boom! You begin to hear talk of falling off the wagon, and they postpone this goal to the next month or year. In the end, it may never again be put in effect.

Is this honestly the right way? Should that one spot dampen all their previous efforts? Studies are showing that they really shouldn't. Although, staying as true as possible to a new routine is necessary, missing a day every so often will not wipe out the progress that you've made so far.

6. Muscle through: In building your will to push through in the event of failure, the common consensus seems to be that the best motivation was "tough love" or being harsh on the backslider (especially if it's yourself). You might see personal trainers, bosses, and life coaches being outrightly insulting all in the name of being firm. While it is always useful to be honest and fully accept blame for missteps, being unnecessarily acrid has been shown to do little more than erode self-confidence.

7. Suck it up: Still, on the topic of being kind, we should set limits. It is a leading notion that, to stick to a habit, one must go above and beyond themselves as a show of commitment to the change. The main reason this one should be debunked is that it can have nasty consequences.

While it goes without saying that you will have to push yourself to some extent (if it was all that easy, a proper approach wouldn't be needed in habit formation), everyone should know when to quit; especially when it comes to physically strenuous activities. Having decided to lift a certain weight, or a set distance daily should come second to reason if you feel unwell.

8. In my genes: As far as excuses go for not putting more discipline into goal achievement, some people prefer to blame it on their predecessors. While it would be ignorant to suggest that there aren't real instances where genetics prevent people from attaining their aims, this claim is usually a case of mistaken identity. When someone says their parents had smoking/weight/fidgeting issues, so they are stuck with the same, ninety percent of the time, this isn't the case.

More often than not, these bad habits are just based on conditioning. The environments we exist in play a large part in what we consider acceptable behavior and what through repetition forms a piece of us. A childhood environment is definitely one of the most relevant, not only since it is the most sensitive stage in development, but also because it tends to be one of the longest periods we spend in a single, constant setting. This means that these types of negative habits can also be modified, but will most likely require more attention (especially in the response phase).

9. Bite the bullet: The final misconception we will analyze is that beginning from the hardest aspect and working your way down is the least stressful method of sticking to a new habit. We are often advised to take on the milestone, and this will make anything else a walkover. Unfortunately, this is another example of trying to use willpower to force the routine. In actuality, an attempt to take on a large chunk of work from the outset is nothing but a way to choke yourself up; chances are, you're not going to do so well with that load, which will do nothing but discourage you, and convince you of imminent defeat.

Avoid all such potential drawbacks on your habit-forming path.

Roadblocks

So, what are the barriers that actually inhibit the process of habit-forming? As it happens, the real culprits are things like:

1. **Procrastination**: The longer you put it off, the less likely you are to get around to it.
2. **Negativity**: How you think determines how far you'll get.
3. **Unconducive environments**: Putting yourself in positions where you know you're exposed to retrogressive triggers.
4. **Impatience**; Routines take time to develop, and getting fed-up after not seeing instant results is, in itself, a bad habit.

5. **Routine abandonment**: Skipping one day on occasion cannot botch up your habit, but becoming slack and not keeping up with it is just a waste of time and energy that leads to empty expectations.
6. **Comparison**: At times, seeing those around us "get their acts together" can encourage a catalyst within our own lives, but monitoring the rate of progress others are making can also be a depreciating factor.
7. **Copying**: As previously stated, having somebody to look up to, or stir in you the enthusiasm for change can be a good thing. What's not as good a thing is when you turn that person's story into a bible or achievement manual. Your progress is likely to be different because of an array of factors, like your personalities, schedules, occupations, and other habits.
8. **Excuses**: While there will be barriers in your path, and times when you feel like giving up on the entire thing, it is in your best interest to persevere.
9. **Been there, done that**: A major excuse of its own can be heard from people who have already tried a number of "solutions" for getting rid of, or taking up their specific habit. To be fair, anyone can understand how potentially irritating it could be to have already put in the work for a goal, to no avail. However, as long as there is still something in yourself that bothers you, it is ultimately worth giving it another shot. The difference now will be working smart and not just hard.
10. **Thought over action**: While emphasis has been rightly placed on the frame of mind with which one approaches any challenge, it is of equal importance to note that habits are based on actions, and without you actually doing the needful for progress, merely thinking "happy thoughts" is no good.
11. **Lack of record**: The objective may be to become virtually unaware of these new parts of our routines, but it has been found to be useful to list out and keep track of milestones in the process of evolution, mainly for inspiration.
12. **Obsession**: Too much of anything will have adverse effects; so, even as you monitor the ups and downs, keep it in the back of your mind not to get overly caught up with every nicety.

The Way Forward

The truth is that altering bad habits is really not as hard to achieve as is the popular opinion. The answers are not in setting far-fetched aspirations, but rather in taking a series of little steps that may end up changing your life.

Beginning today, remember to:

1. Start small: Take things a little at a time, you can't succeed if you never try. Medals are given to those who run the race.

2. Join forces with someone: Many have testified on the efficacy of working to stop/start a habit with a partner. Aside from not feeling like the sole, and isolated culprit who "can't do this, or has to start doing more that," it is good to have someone to discuss with (and complain to) on any challenges faced over the course of change. If you find it difficult to pair with people around, or simply feel a bit ashamed, the good news is that there are all sorts of networks and support groups you could get into contact with where you could connect with someone like-minded in no time.

3. Plan for failure: As positive as we would prefer to be, and as much commitment as we may invest, the truth is, it is wiser to be prepared for slip-ups. This is not some sort of self-debasing activity or a show of lack of faith in yourself; it is just thinking ahead. Being prepared for a worst-case scenario implies that if, and you should mean if, things don't go exactly to plan, we have a backup to instantly implement, instead of laying around feeling guilty or sorry for yourself. Planes with parachutes aren't assuming a crash is inevitable, after all.

4. Celebrate your progress: Every minute win is, in fact, a win, and deserves recognition and reward. It is of the essence to note that your celebration should not run contrary to the goal. What would be the point of rewarding yourself with a bottle of beer, if you're looking to cut down your alcohol consumption?

5. Not buy into "schemes": Everywhere you turn, you see adverts and articles purporting to help you "be twenty times more focused now!," "overcome that addiction instantly!" or "get over laziness in three days!." The brain doesn't form habits in that way. Looking for these shortcuts leads to disappointment; and in cases where "special supplements" are prescribed, it may also result in bodily harm.

6. Take a deep breath: Most importantly, remember that who, or whatever else you're working on these issues for, you are doing it to create a version of you to be proud of first, and for that reason, should avoid anxiety over them at all costs.

Chapter 3: Dangers of Comfort Zones

There are a lot of people out there that love nothing more than being in their comfort zone while there are others that try all they can to make sure that they are not in their comfort zone at all times. You may think that there is no reason why a person would not want to be in his or her comfort zone, but you should know that there are a lot of reasons.

Being in your comfort zone is good and all, but it restricts you from a lot of things. The strange thing about staying in your comfort zone is that when it starts taking a toll on you, you would not be able to realize it until it is too late.

There are a lot of dangers of comfort zones. Some of those dangers include:

1. Fear of taking risks: A lot of people do not like taking risks in the first place, probably because they would not be able to recover from any loss if the risk does not go in their favor or maybe because they are just scared. It is very important to know that taking risks is one of the most essential things you could do for yourself as a human being.

Risks bring you out of your comfort zone and show you things about yourself that you never thought existed. When you are in your comfort zone, you never really know your strengths and weaknesses, your highs and lows, and many more. The fact that you are stuck in the same routine, every day, doing the exact same thing is not going to help you get what you want in any way. All it does is slow you down and hide your full potential, which means that if you do not break out as soon as possible, you may never get your true potential.

2. Limited growth: This is another very important danger of comfort zones. Comfort zones are known to limit growth for as long as you stay in them. For instance, you work in a company where you are paid a substantial amount of money and you feel comfortable there at all times. You should know that you would not want to leave that place as long as you feel comfortable there and there are a lot of other places where you could be paid a lot more for the same work you are doing but just because you feel comfortable there, you would not want to move a muscle.

Just like that, you would be in a particular place for the rest of your life and not grow at all. A lot of people face this same problem but find it hard to know why.

The thing is that the answers they are looking for are staring them right in the face. If they learn to leave their comfort zones once in a while and go out there to see what the future holds, they would definitely see a lot more growth.

3. Routine living: Now this is an aspect that not a lot of people would agree with, but it is so true. If you are the kind of person that follows the exact same routine every single day of the week, there is absolutely no way you are going to be productive at all. You eat at the same restaurant, shop from the same grocery stores, go to work every day using the same routes. When you do all of this every day, there is no way you are going to get to where you are supposed to in life. Why? You are always confined to the same thoughts, activities, and actions at all times.

When you learn to break your routine, you would be able to comfortably think outside the box, and when you are able to think outside the box, you would have a whole lot of good ideas at your disposal at all times. You should know that there are companies that pay people to help them think outside the box. The people they hire are not people that constantly live their lives by routines, these people live their lives with as little planning as possible. That is why they are who they are.

Chapter 4: Decluttering (Helpful to Forming Good Habits)

There is absolutely nothing strange about having some junk lying around in your room, or even leaving your room in a mess once in a while. However, there is definitely something wrong with a person who constantly and frequently allows their home, office, etc., to be filled with junk and other (mostly of little value) items. This could be the result of impulse buying — which in itself is a phenomenon characterized by the unrestrained purchase of unneeded goods, even beyond a person's financial capabilities — to situations where a person holds on to items that they have no use for anymore. Even when the items hold no sentimental value to them.

Decluttering requires, first, a firm resolve to get one's life back on track. To really begin the decluttering process, the person must first realize how the clutter may have been negatively impacting their lives and inhibiting them from moving forward. After that, the person will have to set achievable goals on the decluttering journey, detailing how and when they intend to declutter their personal space.

The next phase usually involves the active decluttering process. "Active," as used here does not suggest that the mental work that goes into preparing for the decluttering is passive. It is anything but. However, the active decluttering process refers to the physical work that is carried out by the person seeking to declutter.

This phase would see the person sorting through their belongings, deciding on the items to keep, the ones to recycle or the ones to give away. This part takes up the bulk of the time of the decluttering process and could be ongoing for several weeks at a time, depending on the size of the clutter.

In a vast majority of cases, a person who has a problem with accumulating items that are often useless has to be wary for the rest of their lives. This is because some factors that lead to clutter could be an addiction (like impulse shopping), and it becomes easy to slip back into bad habits. A person who decides to clutter will have to pay no mind to sunk costs.

A person who contemplates how much they would lose if they give away their items would not do a good job of decluttering. This line of thinking, in itself, is a form of hoarding and, by extension, a way of accumulating clutter. In the same vein, such a person has to keep in mind the items they make use of frequently, the ones they rarely use, and the ones they've outgrown. This sorting system will help the person determine what stays and what goes.

Make no mistake, decluttering is not a pleasant exercise. As a matter of fact, in most cases, it is usually when the person begins to feel the impact of accumulating various items that they even consider decluttering in the first place. In fact, it is often when the person begins flailing that they actually give some serious thoughts to decluttering. The point of this is to establish that decluttering has many inherent benefits, among which is the fact that it works to reduce stress for the individual.

Some researchers have shown that there is a direct correlation between accumulating items and stress, thus, in the converse, reducing personal possessions also reduces stress. Furthermore, it creates more room for the person. It makes available spaces that may have been earlier occupied by clutter.

Finally, it can help a person prepare for their eventual demise. The finality of mortality is something every individual has to grapple with. Decluttering helps a person realize what is important, and also helps them decide what happens to their possessions in the event of their eventual demise.

Particularly, on the subject of forming and sustaining good habits, decluttering can be very useful in various respects. Some of which include:

1. Decluttering gives you a sense of control: This is necessary for the sustenance of good habits. The thing with having a lot of clutter is that it becomes difficult to sort through your belongings. It is not uncommon to discover that it will take such a person forever to locate any particular item that they want at any particular time. As the clutter accumulates, the person begins to feel out of control, and stress sets in, together with the many stress-related ailments that there are. In extreme circumstances also, a life of clutter can lead to such psychological problems as depression and obesity. This is usually in the instance where a person hoards or accumulates food. The person may not be hoarding physical items, and the clutter would not be taking up physical space but will be filling up space in the person's body.

However, decluttering makes a person take charge of their life. In the first instance, a conscious decision to arrange your belongings gives you a massive mental boost and establishes a semblance of control for you. When you move further to carry out the physical exercise, each item you put in their rightful place or decide to discard or give over to charity makes more space, physically and mentally, for you to breathe.

This is essential for the formation of good habits because it is necessary for a person to be in charge of their lives before they can start or continue with good habits. In a lot of cases where people are bogged down by bad habits, it is usually because they feel they lack control over their lives. The bad habit is at the driver's seat of their lives (and they aren't even riding shotgun). The cycle has to be broken for a person to come up from under any self-destructive habit. On the other hand, it will take a person who is self-aware and is in total control of their lives to decide to embrace new habits. The mental stimulation that will help such a person to keep going, even when the proverbial going gets tough, can only be mustered when such a person feels they are in control. Decluttering is able to give people this needed control.

2. Decluttering increases focus: It is the truth that decluttering helps a person maintain a grip on their focus. This sort of decluttering is done mentally, mostly. When a person clears their head of all thoughts and focuses on a single one at a time, they are better able to pay attention to the task at hand. While this kind of decluttering is mainly mental, it can also be informed, and sometimes even precipitated, by actual physical decluttering. Hence, when a person declutters their home, it also helps them declutter their minds, thereby improving their focus.

The development of focus is essential for a person developing a new healthy habit. There are usually a lot of distractions for such a person and there will be a need for a stronger resolve for the person to excel. Since decluttering helps improve focus, it helps the person who is forming new habits.

3. Decluttering can bring about the end of bad habits: Decluttering involves a system of self-awareness, and when a person engages in the exercise, they gain further insight into their personality. They'd be further empowered to detect patterns of destructive habits engaged in and get away from such. For instance, removing the chocolates left in the fridge for over three months would the person realize how much junk they are eating, and they'd be able to make adjustments accordingly.

4. Decluttering builds strength which is essential for sustaining new habits: As earlier pointed out, decluttering might require that the person let go of things they love but which serve no purpose. It is even harder if the item has been with the person for months or even years. It takes a certain level of commitment and strength for anyone to successfully do that.

When you declutter, you build strength in one area which could be exhibited in several other areas, in building habits, for example.

The truth is that decluttering provides immediate benefits to the individual. However, beyond these immediate gains, there are certain other fringe benefits that come with engaging in the practice. The building and sustenance of good habits are one of them. If you are working on developing a good habit, it might be a great idea to try decluttering while you are at it.

Chapter 5: Changing Habits (How to Overcome Bad Habits)

The thing about habits is that they are developed in ignorance and require a lot of work to overcome. But like all habits, they can be changed with determination and consistency. Below are some proven ways to overcome bad habits.

Set Up a System of Punishment

To make overcoming a bad habit easier, try setting up a system of punishment. In doing this, the subconscious mind will be conditioned into avoiding punishment. For instance, if you want to stop swearing, getting a swear jar and finding yourself each time you fall back to the habit can help you change.

No one likes to lose money, especially one they worked hard for, so the sheer thought of losing money so easily over a bad habit can propel change. Conversely, set up a reward system for every time you commit to overcoming your bad habit. A punishment and reward system is a positive motivation to help you manage your habits.

Take Record of Your Progress

Keeping tabs on your progress is key to success in overcoming bad habits. As you progress in your commitment to breaking the habit, write down your progress and find motivation in both your successes and failures. Sometimes, you might find yourself wanting to give up or too tired to continue, but with your progress as a baseline to fall back to, it becomes relatively easy to pick yourself back up and continue.

Set Practical Goals

Tasks become easier when they are broken down into goals. Commit to overcoming bad habits by setting small and practical goals to help you as you go. Also, practicality is needed in your approach because setting standards that are too high will only make you miserable and account for failure. Don't try to overcome a habit in one try. Consider this analogy: while speeding, do you suddenly pull back on the brakes or slowly bring the car to a halt? The latter right? Well, apply the same science to your habits.

Come Up with Reasons to Overcome a Habit

We are all aware of the drawbacks of nurturing bad habits, but sometimes, even this consciousness may not suffice to help us overcome a habit.

This logic also applies in the case of replacing a habit with another one. It often happens that the old habit might have a stronger reward system than the substituting habit, and this might disrupt the process of overcoming the old habit. To deal with this shortcoming, it is imperative that you analyze the effects of a habit and come up with valuable reasons to quit it.

For instance, if you want to quit a habit like nail-biting, knowing how it makes you look, as well as its effect on your health, may help you overcome it. For one, nail-biting disrupts healthy nail formation and can be a pretty embarrassing habit.

Prepare to Be Faced with Challenges

Cultivating good habits is no easy task, so it is imperative that you prepare yourself for whatever difficulties it brings. It is only normal for unforeseen contingencies and temptations to rise and prove inhibitive of your goals, so you must be ready for them. You should understand that these challenges are part of the road to success, and come up with creative ways to deal with them. But, in all things, be determined to quit your bad habits, as that determination will reward you handsomely.

Start by Making Small Changes

Sometimes, going slow in your approach to changing habits might not be enough to overcome bad habits, so you must learn to incorporate small changes as you go too. Overcoming bad habits is challenging, so it's best you are patient with yourself and start with small adjustments here and there rather than opting for dramatic changes. The idea is to ingrain these changes in your subconscious to completely replace a bad habit with a much better one. For instance, if you want to practice eating healthy and curb your sweet tooth, rather than outrightly denying yourself that sugary cup of tea, you can try using much healthier sugars or honey. This way you still get to satisfy your sweet tooth without compromising on your health. Over time, small changes like that become a part of you and replace your bad eating habits.

Recognize Related Habits

A close inspection of habits reveals that some habits have associations with other habits. For instance, sleeping late is tied to waking late and being late to your duties. In this case, the bad habit involved, staying up late, triggers the habit of waking late and tardiness, all of which become chronic habits if one persists. To overcome a bad habit and maintain a good one, you start by finding out about the related habits and curbing them. Without this, the bad habit will inhibit your ability to form healthy habits. You have to sacrifice the habit of staying up late to enjoy the changes in waking up early and being punctual.

Recognize the Reasons Behind a Habit

Identifying the presence of a bad habit in your life is not enough to help you understand or overcome the habit. Recognizing the reason for which a habit occurs can help you avoid its triggers. In this way, you gradually overcome the habit. Having realized its triggers, consider analyzing its effect on you as both a bad and good influence. If the habit has more damaging effects than benefits, it's best you break it.

Maintain a Driving Force

Goals alone will not suffice to help you successfully break up a bad habit. Without a driving force, it is impossible to achieve your goals. Meaning, self-motivation is a core factor for achieving your goals of overcoming a bad habit. If you want to cultivate the habit of exercising every day, you must find a driving force that keeps you on that goal at all times. Without this driving force, getting over a habit becomes arduous work. So, to begin, you would have to set up an alarm system to remind you of your decision to exercise. Avoid keeping the alarm within arm's length to avoid you snoozing it. Getting up to keep up with the habit would be a chore within the first periods, but determination and commitment will see you through. Afterward, it all falls to self-motivation to keep you through the good habit of exercising every day.

Understanding the Triggers of Bad Habits

Knowing what triggers bad habits is not enough to overcome them. You have to understand in detail how the trigger works to be able to stay conscious of it long enough to overcome the habits. The majority of the time, we practice bad habits without our knowledge, making us powerless against changing them. To avoid this, you should stay mindful of the habit loop as well as possible triggers. This will give us an insight into the habit and how to overcome it.

Change the Setting

Doing the same set of behavior in a particular place over time tends to make the environment or scene a trigger to that habit. This can be quite subtle, so you may not readily notice it. Take, for instance, if you sit on the porch to smoke, the porch can become a cue that triggers you to smoke. To overcome this habit, it is imperative that you change your environment and settings, even slightly, as it can help with changes. The 20-second rule can also come in handy when using this technique.

The rule involves delaying bad habits for at least 20 seconds before acting on the urge. To do this, you can try removing the ashtray from the porch, clearing out all the seats, and leaving your cigar box in the closet. This way, when you feel the urge to smoke, your first discovery would be the inappropriate setting of the porch. Also, the distance of your cravings from your current position will make you think twice about acting on your urges.

Spend Time on Yourself

Perhaps it's unclear to you, but you are your greatest investment. As such, it is imperative that you indulge in a constant process of self-development to improve yourself. Let every day be an opportunity to become a better version of yourself. Go to seminars, read books, develop new skills, go out and explore who you are. Overcome your negative habits by believing in your ability to change and not wavering. Work your way to overcoming any bad habit by developing other important habits. Make sure to take all the actions necessary to help you achieve your goals of overcoming your bad habits.

Visualize Yourself

It is a common belief that the more a person spends time picturing themselves having positive habits, the higher the likelihood of sticking to the said habit. Take, for instance, that well-known and celebrated individuals across the world use the technique of visualization in different ways to achieve their success. This is a powerful technique that comes in handy at any point bad should not be overrated for its ability to help overcome bad habits.

Create an Efficient Daily Routine

A major pattern peculiar to people who are in control of their habits is their ability to come up with solid plans that ensure that they are occupied all day, every day, doing only the things they want to do. When most hours of the day are dedicated to doing something, it leaves little to no room for one to return to their bad habits. This way, the habit loop is broken because the mind is engaged at all times, making it invulnerable to habit triggers. Daily routines are even more successful when one makes plans to practice new and better habits at the expense of bad habits.

Maintain Quality Company at All Times

A fact most people are unaware of is the ability of their company to influence them. Everyone is the average of the company they keep. Never underestimate the ability of your company to influence your habits. This explains why bad company can quickly rub off on good people and vice versa. To quit bad habits and adopt good habits, learn to move with people who already practice the habits you want to adopt. In doing this, make conscious efforts to avoid the company of people who trigger your bad habits.

Alter Your Identity

Each time a person smokes, beyond the habit and action of smoking is a much deeper connection called an identity. This identity describes the person as a smoker. For one who has a sweet tooth and eats too much, the action is not simply performed automatically. There is an identity behind it called obesity. What makes overcoming bad habits challenging is the presence of these identities. As people change, they tend to gradually lose parts of themselves in the process. They lose a part of their identities, an action that is no longer performed in real consciousness. The only way out of this is to take out the identity factor from the habit being performed. As such, one should no longer identify as a smoker but one who smokes cigarettes. One should no longer be tagged fat or obese but merely a person that eats too much. One should no longer be called incompetent but one that is merely unable to succeed at something.

When these identities are removed from the infraction, the habit becomes isolated down to the action, and overcoming the habit is relatively easier. Since one neither identifies with the behavior or can be identified by it, it simply turns into something than one does. This serves as a better way to overcome bad habits because change is possible when a positive identity is created in the habits ingrained in one's psyche. When the positive identity is introduced into the fray, the person identified as obese or fat simply becomes identifiable as a healthy person. And since healthy eating habits are typical to healthy people, the change in identity reinforces a different approach to one's eating habits. From this point onward, such a person will begin to behave and eat like a healthy person, tackling the root problem while the effect handles itself.

Chapter 6: Time Optimization

Time optimization refers to the simple process of creating plans and making conscious efforts to manage the time used to carry out certain activities in a bid to improve overall productivity, efficiency, and effectiveness. Time optimization revolves around juggling the many different demands of life ranging from personal commitments and interests to family, social life, and work within the confines of time. The optimal use of time puts a person in a prime position to dictate how time can be spent or managed in performing activities at their own convenience.

A plethora of techniques, tools, and skillsets can be used to aid time optimization, especially when accomplishing certain goals, projects, and tasks having due dates. In an earlier sense, time optimization used to be about work- and business-related activities alone, but over time, the application of the term transcended to include personal indulgences as well. For time optimization to work, it must be engaged in a system. This system refers to a series of methods techniques, tools, and processes designed to make the most of the time. Regardless of the scope of its application, time optimization is an important part of development, in all facets of human life, as it dictates the time and scope of completion. It is also worthy to note that structural and technical disparities in time optimization exist on account of the disparities in the cultural concept of time.

How to Optimize Time

1. Quit multitasking: The majority of people consider multitasking to be an effective method of getting work done easier and faster, but sadly, this isn't necessarily the case. The fact is, concentrating on one task at once increases productivity and speed. Conversely, multitasking inhibits productivity and should not be indulged in as a method of time optimization. Create to-do lists and deadlines to help you stay in tune with work and avoid distractions. This method helps you get better at what you do because you would be actively involved in the process.

2. Change your settings: One of the most efficient methods of increasing your productivity and time optimization is to alter your environment. This could mean clearing your worktop or moving to a quiet and more conducive environment. Sometimes, it could even mean going off to a new environment to clear your head. Altering your settings could also help you improve productive skills that aid with time optimization. For instance, when you feel disoriented or bored, taking a break from your work environment can help put you back on track to use your time well and accomplish your goals.

Another factor to consider in changing settings is the mental and physical effects of the change, as these factors are necessary and contribute to the general success of time optimization both in the short and long term. The environment you change and how much time you spend in it can affect how we use time.

3. Always make work a priority: Before starting the day, it is important that you make a list of everything you hope to achieve on that day, particularly the things that need your attention the most. Unimportant tasks can be time-consuming and that doesn't help with time optimization. There are urgent activities that ought to be finished on the same day while other less important ones can be carried over into the following day(s). This way, the important stuff would be cleared up, leaving time to deal with less important ones.

4. Delegate your activities: It is common for people to take on more activities than they can handle. This is not advisable as it can lead to huge stress and burnout over time. Delegating your activities doesn't mean you are shirking from your duties; rather, it is an important part of time optimization. Mastering the art of delegating work to others and outsourcing work to people based on their abilities and expertise can help promote productivity and good time optimization.

5. Ensure to take breaks regularly: Whenever you feel overwhelmed, stressed out or tired, it is important that you take the time out for about 10 to 15 minutes. Overly stressing yourself has a huge impact on your overall well-being and can disrupt one's productivity. To help master regularly going on breaks, it's best to schedule these few minutes of downtime engaging in activities that help you regain your energy and orientation, as well as distressing. When on your break, try going for walks or listening to calming music. You can also engage in exercises that revitalize the body like yoga and stretches. The best way to spend breaks, however, are with the people you love.

6. Keep away from unhealthy distractions: Distractions are a necessary evil until they begin to interfere with important tasks and time optimization; then they become unhealthy. So, just as there are healthy distractions, there are also unhealthy ones. When distraction takes you from doing valuable work with your time, you will fall behind on your goals and your productivity rate will decline rapidly. As such, it is necessary to know the distractions that eat into your time the most and make conscious efforts to refrain from them. Take for instance, while working, going on social media isn't exactly advisable, except your work depends on it. Otherwise, owing to how addictive it can be, it can constitute a distraction and eat into your time and productivity. And even when you're not directly on these platforms, staying connected in the background serves as a potential form of distraction, because you may be one notification short of wasting lots of time.

7. Plan your activities: Walk around with a notebook or planner in which you make a list of every task that comes to mind. Before the start of any day, make sure you always have a to-do list ready. Make the important activities your primary concern. But doing that alone wouldn't help. You have to be sure that the tasks are practical and can be performed within a reasonable timeframe. For better optimization of time, it's best to make three lists to cover your personal, home or social, and work life.

8. Early beginnings: The one thing successful people have in common is that they make early starts to their days. This way they are better able to visualize and effectively plan how the day would turn out. The reason for this is not far fetched: in waking up early, you are in a relatively calmer, more creative, and more clear-headed state than ever. As the day goes by, the law of diminishing returns kicks in and your energy levels start to drop considerably. Over time, productivity is affected as well, leading to inefficiency in time optimization.

9. Put your downtimes to good use: This technique is quite tricky given that downtimes are an essential part of time optimization, so balance is required. Spending all your downtimes prioritizing and planning your day is quite bad and can result in so much stress it could cause burnout. Albeit, should you find yourself with some extra downtime, nothing is wrong with making the most of it. For instance, getting stuck in traffic affords you extra minutes to your downtime between tasks. You could use this period to make up your mind on how to spend your evening or what to make for dinner. While waiting for your turn in a queue, you can use the time to calculate your monthly expenses and calculate your savings. Opportunities like these are ones that account for smart use. So, it's not as though you're indulging yourself when you ought to rest, you're simply capitalizing on contingencies.

10. Create deadlines: Whenever you have things to do, setting up realistic deadlines and sticking to them can help you optimize your time. Setting up deadlines a few days before taking on another task can help you optimize your time on clearing previous and existing tasks before then. Also, deadlines can serve as challenges that motivate you towards better time optimization. Ensure to set up a reward system for every time you meet a deadline, no matter how small.

Why Indulge in Time Optimization?

Why should you optimize your time? The answer is simple: time optimization aids you in staying ahead of commitments and getting more done in the best and quickest way possible. But there's more to it than that. The concept has a plethora of benefits that cut across all facets of human life. While it might seem demanding, it really isn't and only demands a reasonable level of discipline. Also, the benefits of time optimization far outweigh the effort it requires.

Below are some of the benefits of time optimization.

1. More time to yourself: Not only is time optimization capable of decreasing stress and anxiety, but it also affords you more free time to spend however you want. Mastering the art of engaging only important tasks, or regulating, outsourcing, and getting rid of unnecessary tasks, you free up time on your schedule. It's kind of like decluttering your life.

2. Using up less time: Good optimization of time decreases inappropriate use of time. We spend the majority of our time on less important tasks, and although they may seem urgent, they hold no value in the long or short term. In other cases, they are not a part of your goals and priorities and could act to the contrary. Also, we tend to use up valuable time trying to figure out the tasks to engage in and getting things set up, all of which time optimization helps take care of efficiently. This doesn't imply that more is done alone. No. It helps to clear off tasks from your plans, which are unnecessary and contribute no value to you whatsoever.

3. Aids in focusing on priority tasks: It is common for people to classify their loved ones as one of their priorities in life, as well as some areas of their lives, but their actions betray this claim, sadly. The majority of these people use up way too much time at work, and they become stressed out and overwhelmed to indulge any of their said priorities. Also, some of them go as far as bringing home their work and putting in extra hours. Although this is sometimes a case of misplaced priorities, with others, it is a case of poor time optimization. And if the latter party used their time well, their claims would be utterly right and unquestionable.

4. Decreased level of procrastination: Time optimization allows you to get more out of your day. By setting up schedules and to-do lists, you set out the tasks you want to achieve in a day and attain a subconscious awareness of what you ought to get done. Planning tasks allows you to comprehend when a time ought to finish, as well as the amount necessary to complete the task. In doing this, planning enables time optimization by eradicating the struggles of wondering what task to tackle first, while also ensuring no task goes forgotten. By planning each day, you will be able to avoid procrastinating because you are more likely to adhere to tasks when they are written down. Staying accountable to your daily activities ensured that they are completed in the quickest way possible.

Although it seems relatively inexplicable how planning and scheduling can allow for flexibility, it isn't the case with time optimization. A knowledge of what tasks are best-completed aids a person in knowing how much free time one is allowed in a day.

Chapter 7: The Benefits of Adopting Good Habits

Often times, we are told that to succeed in life we need a strategy, patience, guts, commitment, and other qualities. A lot of the time, none of those listed contain good habits as a requirement for success. This is quite sad because no one really gets ahead in life without them.

Thus, it is no surprise that most people give up easily after many attempts at getting a particular work done, and they are also often plagued with such self-sabotaging ills as laziness, procrastination, and other obstacles. In the midst of all these, we rarely see the role that our habits play in getting us to the places we want to be or stopping us from getting where we want to be.

You might have had conversations with friends or acquaintances who tell you they will get this or that done by the end of that month or year and they actually get it done and you wonder, how were they able to accomplish that? Perhaps you tried it and it didn't work out and also it didn't seem as though any other person could do it.

We all know how frustrating and discouraging all these can be. The truth is that those goals are actually very achievable. It all depends on the habits you have, over time, built for yourself. It is for this exact reason, and far many more, which will be discussed in this chapter, that we ought to take good habits very seriously. They are often difficult to get into, but, thankfully, not impossible to acquire.

1. **The right habits help you get to your goals**: However tiny our goals are, they are still our goals. We all always have goals that we constantly set for ourselves to get through with at the end of any period. It could be to buy a house, get a best-selling book published, start a business, grow a business, or even get into school.

   They are all goals and they matter so much that if you do not take them seriously and build the right habits to get them achieved, you would be at the same spot at the end of the period you set to have accomplished your goals. Big goals do not happen overnight. Your good habits are very important here. Good habits will get you through. They are activities that have become consistent, automatic, and less complex for you to get into.

Good habits not only get you started but, above all, they keep you going and on the right track too. With the right habits, you are better off. You are more efficient, productive, effective, and strategic about your thoughts and actions. All these cannot be separated from the important traits you need to get your good work done properly.

2. **The right habits allow you to help the people around you**: Your worth is the subtraction of your bad deeds from your good deeds. The amount of these good deeds determines exactly how many persons around you you get to help and impact. It also determines exactly how much help you get for yourself in times of your needs.

   As the CEO of a company or any head of an organization or business, your team follows your lead. Do you know that as a parent, your morals and the things you do and say are imitated by your kids? These form the larger part of how your children will grow into responsible adults? Psychology even shows that, in relationships, couples, after some time, begin to act, talk, and think like each other.

   They eventually pick up most, if not all, of each other's habits. Look at the most common characteristics of cultures, communities, sports teams, and you will find that they have been built from constantly interacting with each other. We cannot deny the fact that what we do regularly, our good habits, can and will influence the people around us.

   Getting to influence people around us depends totally on how many good habits we have imbibed. Developing good habits is, therefore, the surest way to boost your relationship with the people around you. More importantly, as a leader, there isn't a better way to, as they say, lead by example.

3. **The right habits can help boost the overall quality of your life**: There is something called keynote habits. These are habits whose impacts can affect more than one aspect of your life. They are targeted at achieving a particular thing, but they eventually help you achieve a lot more than you aimed at getting.

   These habits are usually correlated to other habits so that significant improvements in one aspect can give you a boost in other aspects. Let us take a look at the very good example of exercising. We exercise, majorly because we want to attain good health and, of course, stay fit at the same time.

Overall, the habit of good and constant exercise helps us improve our productivity, energy management, time management, and mental health. Bear in mind that these additions are not usually what we set out to get when we engage in exercise. When you get into two or more good and healthy habits, they help you create a routine for your life and goals. It is these routines that we go through every day, which help us to be more efficient and productive on a consistent basis. According to Aristotle, we are what we repeatedly do; excellence is therefore not an act but a habit.

4. **With the right habits, you reap lifelong benefits**: You cannot change your life until you change something you do daily and as such, the secret of your success is found in your daily routine. Some benefits have been mentioned above, and they are not just one-time things.

Engaging in positive habits continuously and frequently will produce results that are not just beneficial but lasting. Forget the fleeting satisfaction of feeling like a "good person." What is being described here is a drastic change to your character that will impact your chances at happiness a great deal.

As was mentioned at the beginning, you will feel more accomplished knowing that you have drilled the right habits into getting what you want, and, when eventually you do not get these things, you are comfortable knowing you did your best. You will develop self-discipline in the process, and you will be more intentional. The benefits of having the right habits will live with you for years to come.

5. **With good habits, you can become that person you most want to be**: When you think of all the successful business owners, millionaires, writers, and CEOs, they sure did not get to that enviable position easily or instantly. It was gotten from years of hard work and, of course, developing the right habits.

You can bet that even in their trying times – when they never felt like showing up, being seen, or when they failed – they still showed up regardless and fought for what they wanted. They had the best of habits to lead them through it all. Instead of cramming a bunch of motivational quotes, becoming a better person can be a lot easier if you surround yourself with the right routines and develop very good habits. Unlike fleeting motivation, good habits are more dependable. Habits are sustainable and get you through, whether you are fired up or not.

6. **Good habits replace motivation**: We all, at one point or the other, go through that stage when we do not want to do anything: eat, exercise, or even go to work. But the bad aspect is building these acts into habits.

   When these things become habits, they become really difficult to break. It becomes difficult to get anywhere near our goals. They become as natural as breathing. Looking at it the other way, when we make an effort to gradually build the right habits into our lives, they become natural to us as breathing is. Thus, even when you do not have the motivation to carry out any actions, habits can get you on your feet. We are better off for it at the end.

7. **Good habits are a sure bet to your foundation for life**: You are your daily habits. Your habits become you and they eventually set the tone for your life. What you choose to make a priority in your life will be instrumental in shaping you into what you want to become, or oppositely, what you do not want to be.

   If you develop the habit of conversing with people around you with joy, daily, it becomes an important part of you. If you get used to chatting with your children daily, you create a bond with them. If you decide to eat veggies more often, then you will be making a decision to look and be more healthy. What you choose to become will materialize when you build strong and good habits around you.

Anything worth celebrating over or accomplishing does not materialize overnight. It is never about what you do once in a blue moon, but about what you do consistently, habitually, and daily. How do you spend your days? At the very beginning, learning good habits can be very difficult, and it sure should be.

It's more like an old woman learning how not to slouch. It is difficult but not entirely impossible. Developing the right habits will go a long way to help you achieve what has been discussed above. It will, ultimately, get you to where you want to be while reducing the time spent doing things that do not, in the grand scheme of things, matter. Set your goals, set your behavior chain, and hang in there no matter what.

Chapter 8: Daily Guide to Changing Habits

The first question one should ask here should probably be, "How many days does it take to change one's habits from bad to good?" Well, it shouldn't take you more than 30 days to get yourself into a changed person with better habits. We all definitely want to get our work done and effectively, habits are practically the most beneficial in this sense.

This chapter will be subdivided to help understand how 30 days can lead to changing your habits for good.

Willpower Not Motivation

Many people have wondered if it is actually possible to form a new habit in 30 days. The answer is yes. There are, in fact, experiments to prove this. Getting a new habit may not be as easy – or enjoyable – as eating. Even that could be hard because there's some work necessary to lift the food and put it in your mouth.

The point is this: learning a new habit is not easy, and if you're really going to stick to the 30 days therapy, then it's going to require much more discipline. It's normal to struggle when forming new habits and it's expected to lose motivation in the process. I'd love to ask you some questions though: how many times have you really tried to get out of bed early? How many times have you tried to keep your inbox clean from junk? How many times have you tried to dine on healthy foods and not junk?

It's not enough that you doubt your ability to get to your target of new habits in 30 days, you may not have even given it a shot yet. Here is the thing: we have people around us who managed and are still managing to overcome really arduous tasks in very short periods of time. It can take a person just one crucial moment to let go of smoking and drinking. It could take another week or month.

It can take just seeing something for a person to decide to start feeding daily on healthy food and not junk. It can take another person a flash to begin to write every day and then eventually finish that one novel they have written for years.

If we genuinely tell ourselves the truth, these examples are around us. These people are those whose everyday life we get glimpses of. A lot of people and experiments have doubted the 30 days theory, and it has affected the way people see the instant change in habits for people who decide to stick with their rules of changing themselves for the better. The evidence for the success of the 30 days theory is scattered all around us as we will soon learn.

Why do most people not believe that it's possible to get into very good and healthy habits in 30 days? Some folks have taken the pain to prove that the 30 days theory is only a myth and that it takes about a year to really form new habits and have them become a part of you. In truth, the 30 days theory of habit formation is *not* a myth as will be explained step-by-step below.

The 30-Days Habit-Formation Guide

To form a new habit, three key things must come into play: your level of commitment, your internal and external accountability, and the type of habit. As has been mentioned earlier, getting a new habit is not easy but it is possible. If you want the 30 days habit-formation strategy to work out, then acknowledging that it's not going to be easier should be the first step. You will have to decide what, how, and why something is important to you.

Ask yourself: if I do this today, what difference will it make to my day? How will that habit help me achieve my goals, short and long term? How will this impact my relationship with everyone around me? Once these questions are asked, you would have to formulate your answers to these questions in an emotionally captivating manner, in such a manner that gives a new narrative to who you are. A better version of your former self. It is more like giving life to the new habit you have formed for yourself. This narrative should remain with you daily.

Tell yourself this narrative before going to bed; it reminds you of the new person you have become. The better person you have built yourself into. This mental exercise becomes the psychological glue with which you will stick the new habit. To ensure that you do not constantly drift from your course, you have to add sounds and sensations of touch or smell to your narration. You should say to yourself: I am a writer. I am rich. I am an early riser. What you are doing is living the result you are yet to see. You want to develop the habit of constantly reading or rising early or writing every day, then it is enough that you identify yourself with who you are working to become. You are only telling yourself to work more on the skills that would help you get to where you want to be. The stronger your reasons for your new habits, the more likely and faster you are going to develop them. On the other hand, bland and non-captivating stories do nothing for you. They do not help you build your imagination about where you want to be or who you want to become. It is more likely that with unimaginative narratives that you will most likely forget the reason you decided to pick up that habit in the first place. This will happen because the story you have told yourself is not captivating enough and does not reflect what you want to become enough for the story to stick.

Accountability Plan to Form a Habit in 30 Days

You need an accountability mechanism to stand you out from the person who has merely built just imaginative stories about themselves. You will need an internal accountability mechanism through your conscience, and an external accountability mechanism through social support groups or a coach or mentor. The better these systems are, the more likely you are to achieve all you want. Otherwise, you are better off without the accountability mechanisms.

To hold yourself accountable, it is important that you become closer to your own self. Become your own best friend. Treat yourself the way you would a best friend because we often wish good things for our friends, do the same for yourself. This way, you will most likely want to always encourage yourself and all your efforts. This will also help you remind yourself to stay on track and keep focus. You hold yourself accountable without any atom of bitterness from failing to reach your goals or falling back once in a while from the 30 days new habit formation.

Your accountability to yourself will be borne from a place of care and love for yourself. This is way better than the policy of conditioning yourself to do things you most likely do not want to do. Such an approach can be quite counterproductive, and you might achieve nothing at the end of the day. You must not do it all on your own, remember. In fact, it is way more difficult doing it on your own.

As was discussed above, you should join support groups and get mentors to see you to your goals. Most people prefer to work with professionals, and so coaches are recommended because they give you a step-by-step guide on what to do and how to better do them.

Determining the Size of the Habit You Want to Form Is Vital

The size of your goal will determine if you will develop a new habit within 30 days. If your target habit is like running a marathon then you can't get that in 30 days. Or if the new habit you are trying to develop is writing at least 2000 words of fiction every day then, 30 days might be too small, especially if you have no skills in writing. The best way to achieve big goals will be to break your large habits into mini-habits. These are habits that can be achieved at least in a day.

Breaking your large goals into mini-habits makes them more achievable. Let's take the goal of wanting to write at least 2,000 words of fiction every day as an example. The best thing to do in such a situation will be to get yourself to write every day without setting any word limit for yourself. It could be 50 words or 100, but make sure to write fiction every day. It is only when you are able to commit to the small things that you can get your head around the big things.

Ultimately, the same would go for the marathon example we have above. You could simply start running every day. Just run without any desire to go through many struggles or reach a benchmark. Once you are comfortable with running every day then you can take this habit up notch like running quarter of a marathon and then gradually you can form the habit of running a marathon every day.

An Effective Strategy for Habit Formation

There is something called the "Habit Graduation Strategy." This is the strategy used to build habits over time and then automate them. Here, you are expected to see your 30-days habit formation as a work in progress and not as a do-or-die affair. You only have to take small but consistent actions every day and then gradually build up a new habit. The most important thing to start with is that you start with something small and not too challenging and then from there you can up the challenge.

Resolve to do something a little more challenging than the previous thing you have been doing every day. You will also need to make sure that you continue this new challenging habit every day. Keep taking the challenge higher until you reach your goals. So, for example, instead of promising yourself you would run on the field for 30 minutes every day, you could start with just running 10 minutes every day.

Get used to doing it and then start taking it higher. 11 minutes the next day, 12 minutes the day after that and on and on. You should learn to restrain yourself from running more than the number of minutes you have fixed for each day. The reason for this is to prevent yourself from easily wearing out from doing too much of what you should not be doing at a time. Take it slowly and gradually until you get what you want. Be very consistent.

Remember to reflect on your progress and also be consistent about it. If you take in more than you can chew at a time, then you might lose the motivation to continue. If you have an issue with moving your challenge up or, to put it more aptly, changing from 10 minutes to 11 minutes and, eventually, 12 minutes, then you could just always up the challenge by just 30 seconds instead of a full minute. It will be slower to get to your goal this way, but knowing what works for you and doing exactly that helps you retain your motivation and pace on your journey to build a new habit.

What to Expect on Your 30-Days Habit-Formation Plan

You might be wondering how your habit creation life will switch or happen within the next 30 days of forming this new habit. Here is what you are likely to go through in the next 30 days of your habit formation.

Days 1-6

This is where your motivation level is at the highest point. You are enthusiastic about getting into your new habit. Your habit is the best thing to you in the world; it matters so much to you that you are always into it. From this stage upwards, it could get really demanding.

Days 7-13

This is the stage where most people quit the most. They find this stage too challenging and everyone cannot deal with this stage successfully and move on to the next. What do you do? Go back to scratch where you told your story in an emotional and captivating manner. Get images and videos and quotes and try to tell your story again with them. What you should be doing within these days is to reinforce into your imagination what you want to do and how you want it done. Be assured that once you pass this usually difficult stage, what follows is less challenging.

Days 14-19

Here, please do not rest on your laurels just yet. The major task you have at this stage is to see how much you have fared. You have to note how much difference the habits you have been practicing has made to your body. You could choose to talk about it publicly as a way of noting how the changes have occurred and what it has done to your body and your mind. Alternatively, you could choose to just write them down. You are, by now, 1/3 of the way, and it's more like a mid-way celebration.

Days 20-26

Here, you should start marking your calendar off to know how many days are left for you to finish your course. Marking off each day helps you feel good about how much you have achieved and how far you have come to attaining your goal of developing a new habit. It also helps to reinforce your motivation since you are almost done. This is like 2/3 of the course done. Well done.

Days 27-30

At this stage, your habit should already have become a part of you. What you should majorly be doing here is how to ensure that this built-in habit does not leave you after the 30-days journey. You could try focusing on the long-term benefits of continuing this new habit and also look at how far you have come with the new habit, and of course, how better you have become. Focus on all the advantages you aimed at getting through the development of this new habit, and if there is, in fact, any advantage you have noticed so far, it will help you keep up beyond the 30days.

Chapter 9: More Willpower vs. Motivation

Our brain is our major decision-maker. It has the ability to choose what we most often want to do as opposed to what we are forced to or not interested in doing. The evolved brain is our angel, and our angel is fueled by our willpower. We are often faced with challenges that affect our focus on our goals. When we are faced with these situations, it is far better that we make decisions that will help us keep in mind the situation of things while also ensuring that we are making decisions that are consistent with what we want in our lives.

No matter how much we design habits into our daily lives, we cannot avoid the importance or impact of willpower in getting us where and what we really want, ultimately. There are three major types of willpower that the brain uses to help us do what we really want.

- **I will power**: this is that power that motivates everyone irrespective of their not wanting to do anything. It is the power that helps us go through tough things to help us accomplish our goals. It is this willpower we use to clean our homes and go out even when we do not want to. It is this willpower that we use to workout.
- **I won't power**: this is the power we call on to resist temptations. It is what gets us to not do those things we crave to do but which we cannot do because of our health or some deformity we are trying to correct. Examples of when this willpower comes to play is when we resist the urge to eat chocolates, play the next episode on Netflix, or hold from saying rude things to a client that was rude.
- **I want power**: of all the three willpowers discussed above, this is the most important of all the willpowers. It is the willpower that houses our memory. It helps us remember our long-term goals and also helps us to keep track of our goals and desires. What do you really want? Your "I Want Power" helps you keep track of this. It helps us remember and keep track of why we are always exercising every morning. It helps us remember how much of something we want to be.

Unlike the other two types, this one can be produced practically out of thin air. Under this type of willpower, it only takes listening to a motivational speaker or reading inspirational quotes for you to get that rush of energy to want to change your life or become a better person and change the whole world. It is this part of the brain that is cultivated when we want a change in behavior.

Our willpower is what helps us grow our new habit. So, as against motivation, willpower is the most important and most helpful. The next question is: how do you train that part of your brain we described as an angel and strengthen your willpower?

The Willpower Approach

Under the willpower approach, or put more clearly, to better strengthen our use of willpower to develop our new habits, then three strategies should be considered.

1. **Automating goal pursuit**: When we talk about automating your goals, dedication, setting triggers and remembering your overall goal are really important. The idea is to automate your dedication to your goals instead of automating your behaviors. This could be like setting reminders every day to keep you on track on what you plan to do. You could also write down your goals so as to increase your self-awareness of what you need to do.

   When you focus only on your behavior then if there is a change in your environment then you lose pace on what will help you focus on. It's more like having plans in place to run 10minutes every morning and then losing track of that and not doing it at all because, perhaps, you travel to a place where it is more difficult to wake up early like you usually do.

   Who says you can't run when you want to? You can run whenever you decide to get off your bed, just make sure you eventually run. In the previous example, if your goals were automated, there is a higher likelihood that you would wake up earlier.

   Also, automated goals make it that there will be a higher likelihood that you will take a shot at eating the healthiest foods even though you are not with your tracker or coach. You could make a decision to keep track of your weight with automated goals, and so on.

Whatever idea you ultimately come up with, automated goals will help you come up with cues on how to better your condition, even with a change in the environment.

2. **Building the muscles**: It might sound strange when we mention that our willpower is actually our muscle, but it is. In the process of building our new habits, we often face temptations; however, when we make a conscious effort to say no, then we will be building our willpower. The converse will be the case when we try to adjust our new-formed habits to fit into a new environment we have moved into.

   An example is returning to eating chocolates because you now have chocolate stores all around you in your new environment, more than you did in your old environment where you had built a little resistance against chocolates. Just like when we do not exercise and go to the gym, we become less fit. It works the same way for with willpower. Our resolve gets weaker when we do not strengthen it.

3. **Make commitments**: This is like being in a relationship. When you decide to get into a relationship with someone, you will definitely want to be faithful to them. If you really decide to stick with someone, then you will stay committed to them come what may.

   Of course, you might go through periodical temptations, but you still make attempts to make sure your relationship with the person works. Usually, all that is required is a belief in the higher and latter purpose of the relationship.

   Now, this is similar to building your habits through willpower; you oftentimes get doubts. It is worse if the doubts are not only from within but are also coming from the public. "Do you really think you can work out every day? I know you too well, you cannot," and other derailing comments are part of the temptations that make us want to relent on becoming better.

   This tip has been shared earlier in this book: you should develop a new habit by trying to make yourself your own best friend. You will look out for your best friend and encourage them even when the world sees them as unable to accomplish a target. Since here you are your own best friend, you will encourage you, with love and care and strive forward irrespective of what people say about you or your goals and new habits.

All you need, as it relates to your habit-building, is to search for some purpose to your being. You need a higher purpose to help you get through the stages of temptations and disbelief. Make the commitment to see your new positive habits through, regardless of the many hurdles you have to jump. It is during this difficult time that you discover the extent of your willpower.

There are scientific experiments that have shown that willpower and not motivation helps you pull through in building a new habit. Let's look at some.

Experiment 1: The Marshmallow Experiment (3)

The Stanford Marshmallow experiment is probably the most famous willpower experiment. This test deals with the possibilities of succeeding in future and prolonged gratification. The way the experiment worked is that children were given marshmallows (and some got other kinds of foods). They were simply told that if they could delay in eating the food for just 15 minutes or more, then they would certainly get double of whatever was given to them the first time.

The children's results were recorded and kept for many years, which was used to subsequently track these children. Those whose level of willpower was very high (that is those who waited 15 minutes or more before they finally ate was given to them) ended up doing very well in many areas of their lives. They had tendencies of better job performances, had lower incidences of drug abuse, and also higher scores in standardized tests while in college.

Many were in doubt as to whether future successes of the kids could be predicted from something as simple as a marshmallow experiment, but it turned out that it could be. The test was repeated over a variety of students who were further tracked and the results turned out the same.

In the future permutations, the researchers tried to tip their scale a little bit higher by trying to see if a person without willpower could be taught willpower. Can you teach a child to resist having their most wanted snacks for just 15 minutes after it has been given to them? This is what led to the latter experiment we will be discussing. We are about to find out that willpower can actually be strengthened.

Experiment 2: The Radish Experiment

Once researchers knew that it was possible to strengthen willpower, they wanted to know the limit of that strength or possibility. Specifically, they wanted to take a test on what was known as ego depletion. Ego depletion is a drop in willpower and the zeal to forge a new habit or behavior pattern. This is what leads to the constant drop in following through with the benchmarks we set for ourselves when it comes to habit change. Put more simply, depletion occurs when a person loses the ability to regulate their actions, feelings, and thoughts.

The experiment followed this thread: three random groups of people were picked and then each group was asked to solve a complicated puzzle. Each group was given the same puzzle, in different rooms and with different access to different things. Group One was the control group. This group was asked to get to the puzzle without any food given to them. Group Two was placed in a hall filled with so many goodies and foods, and they were told they could take anything they wanted.

Group Three was brought into the same room with those in Group Two, but they were restricted to just the radishes. The import of this is that Group Three had to exert more willpower to stay away from eating comfort meals. They all worked on the puzzle and both the control group and the group placed in the banquet hall (specifically, Group Two, the "you can have anything you want to group," merely worked on the puzzle for about 20 to 25 minutes before giving up.

The "radish group" only lasted for about 8 to 10 minutes before giving up. This was a statistical huge puzzle that showed that those who made use of their "willpower reservoir" to stay away from the comfort meals were less capable of working on the complicated puzzle.

There have been diverse studies conducted on willpower and lots of studies are still going. Most, if not all, of these studies showed that we have a limited amount of willpower but that this limited amount can nevertheless be strengthened.

When the subjects were used for an experiment with their willpower as an implementation intention, they eventually reduce the stress they are likely to face with upcoming tasks.

This reduction in stress increases their chances of future success. It means that if you regularly create triggers on how you respond to certain situations, then you'll be far more likely to stick to a new habit than if you did not. When you fail at something, it doesn't mean you are bad or weak or that you are condemned to failure. You might eventually find out that your willpower often breaks down in one area only because you are very good in another area and are busy doing great things in that other area.

Chapter 10: Disruptors Ahead! Beware!

As you build your habits, there is a high likelihood that you would constantly be faced with distractions and negative energies. It is important that we recognize these disruptors and also give points on how to better curb such.

1. **Alcohol and cocaine**: Cocaine and alcohol are some of the most common types of drug combinations that drug users often abuse. For those who are working on their habits, it is not surprising that most try to combine this because of the results it is likely to produce in the body.

    Cocaine and alcohol have the possibility of increasing one's alertness, blood pressure, and heart rate. According to scientists, who discourage the intake of these drugs when trying to learn something new or achieve a goal, the major reason why most people take this is to ensure that they get a faster result while being oblivious of the stages it took to make the progress. It gives you the feeling of wanting to sleep in a mansion, as though it could be achieved by just sleeping and waking up to find one's self in a mansion. But it never lasts. Mixing cocaine with alcohol helps to produce what is known as cocaethylene which is the major producer of intense pleasure. The side effects of this combination are that it could lead to heart attack, overdose, or death.

2. **Heroin and Alcohol**: The combination of these two drugs gives you the same effects as that of alcohol and cocaine. The most dangerous risk that depressants cause to the body is that it causes slower breathing, and it makes it very dangerous for such a person to stay in a stuffed area for too long. Heroin is a highly addictive drive, and the side effects it causes can be very threatening. Because heroin is highly addictive, it becomes very difficult to quit, and it is for this reason that it is not advisable for you to engage in the intake of these depressants while in the process of becoming a better person. The only thing it does is to blind you from your troubles without really taking them away. It can be frustrating to try and develop a new, and better habit and not succeed, but it is never an excuse to engage in the intake of drugs. They take you farther away than you were when you decided to change your habits for the better.

3. **Ecstacy and alcohol**: Ecstasy is a stimulant, and its adverse effects are usually so serious, especially when it is used with other substances, that

it makes you consume large amounts of alcohol within a very short period of time. This can lead to extreme dehydration and diarrhea together with other side effects such as excessive sweating, heat stroke, nausea, and vomiting.

4. **Sleeping pills and alcohol**: On its own, there are diverse risks of taking sleeping pills. However, when it becomes combined with alcohol, then its side effects become threatening and irreparable, most of the time. Taking the smallest amount of alcohol with sleeping pills can increase its sedative effects and this can affect the system. It is never advisable for anyone to drink large amounts of alcohol with anything containing opioids, anxiety pills, or sleeping pills. Anxiety pills taken with alcohol are also often taken by those working to achieve their goals at very short notice. All of these drugs mentioned above are sedatives, and they can cause real disaster to the respiratory system, the eyes, and most times it causes death.

The side effects of alcohol and drugs on your body can not be overemphasized. Some effects may be minor and only last for some time but some effects are for life and most times, victims have to live the rest of their lives struggling through medications. Whatever the situation is, it is never enough to indulge in drugs to get into a better habit. You can do it without drugs.

5. **Negative friends**: When you decide to build your habit and your goals, it is important that you determine for yourself, the kind of friends that you surround yourself with. Negative friends have a serious effect on your confidence level, your dreams, and how you relate with other people around you. If all they do is to tie you down to something you would rather not do, then you have to let them go. Let's look at some of the reasons and advantages of cutting off negative friends from you.

   a. **You basically become like the first five people you spend most of your life with**: The old saying that suggests that you act and behave just like the first five people you spend most of your time with is not wrong. If the majority of people you surround yourself with are negative people, then you'll most likely begin to feel negative and inferior. You will most likely also see negativity in others. The funny truth in this is that you see your friends like the good ones while you see others as the very bad and discouraging ones. Surrounding yourself however with positive and successful people, boost your zeal to want to achieve your goals.

b. **If you find yourself always being supported by the majority, then it's time to rethink a lot of things**: Have you ever noticed the division between those who follow the crowd and those who follow their own paths? Well, follow your own path. The danger of moving with the majority is that it shrinks your voice and does not give you the platform to really be who you want to be or who you truly are. The point is this: if you have been following the majority of people, then you will have to rethink your steps and decisions. Many of us make decisions based on what everyone is doing at that particular time without thinking of what they are capable of doing on their own, separate from the crowd.

Chapter 11: Don't Impose

You have your new habit, and congratulations, but your habits are yours and it could be quite irritating when you try to make people deal with the new person you have become at all costs. There is a story about this. A woman moved to a book shop counter with just four books in her hand. She had obviously picked out the four books in the bookshop as what she wanted to read. The attendant was new, and she is the one who loves reading, but had for some time been grasping with the inability to read as much as she wants to or buy new books.

So, she had previously placed herself on a habit-changing train and had come out successful. She loved books, and she could read as much as she wanted and get as many books as she wanted too. Back to the woman at the counter. The four books in her arm cost just 4 dollars. The attendant wanted to help her so she offered to give her 10 books for 5 dollars. The woman should be excited right? But, well, she wasn't.

She merely repeated that all she wanted were those four books she was with and nothing more. The woman left with four books and paid 4 dollars. The attendant was surprised and disappointed. She felt the woman didn't know the value of books and that, perhaps, she hadn't convinced the woman enough to want to get new books. The thoughts moving through the attendant's mind were: why was she so unreasonable? Why didn't she just take the offer? It would have been way easier for her. What's her problem?.

We all have been guilty, countless times, of imposing the new person we have worked ourselves into becoming, on others, but it never seems to do much good. The less we try to force people to accept our own view and pattern of living, the better for us. It didn't even occur to the attendant in the example above that perhaps the woman just didn't have enough money on her or perhaps she just didn't love books as much as the attendant did, or better still, perhaps she was buying those books for someone who had specifically mentioned that they needed just those four books.

The more we try to force people to see things the way we see it, the weaker our bonds and relationships with people become and this ultimately affects the manner in which people see us. Instead of forcing someone to accept your own version of what you feel is good for them based on your new-found habit, then it will be way better for both parties if you simply tried to understand their own view of the world. Everyone won't love books, deal with that. Everyone won't love to work out, deal with it. Everyone won't love to stop eating junk food just to get healthier (perhaps they don't have as much willpower as you do), deal with that too. Below are three reasons why you should not try to impose your habits on others.

1. It can make people feel that you do not understand them or care to understand them: Imagine my favorite color is now grey after I got the recommendation to avoid sharp colors from a doctor because of my eyes. Oh well, I bought a grey car and it looks really pretty to me. My friend gets a blue car, and I feel it's ugly and try to tell her that. I tell her never to bother that I would repaint it to grey for her. Bills on me. But she doesn't want it — blue being her favorite color, much like the newfound love I now have for grey. Imagine the kind of animosity my insistence would create.

   The more you try to force your behavior, faith, or values on others, the more marginalized the other person will feel. From the example above, the woman who had been convinced to get more books must have had a bad experience because she never went to that store again. She had been convinced and told why she should buy this number and not this number of books that she had begun to doubt her own sense of judgment, and that is bad for a person.

   It is without a doubt that no one likes to interact with people who try to shove their habits down their throats. The experience could be really damaging, as it makes you feel nothing you ever do is right. It feels like handing over your control and autonomy to someone else while you sit dependent on nothing. You don't like that because no one loves to be pushed around, so don't do it to others.

2. Imposing your habits on others is never an effective strategy to change people's minds or behavior patterns: If you really want someone to accept your way of life and point of view, then you must first respect their own way of living. Respect their habits and behavior and values. Remember that there is a huge difference between respecting someone else's behavior and following their behavior.

   It does not necessarily mean that in respecting someone else's behavior that you allow things that will be harmful to your own being. It's okay to accept people for who they are if this will not affect your character negatively. Even if you feel that it will, then you just have to mention it to them a couple of times. If they choose to remain with that particular harmful behavior, do not think twice about cutting them from your life. It's not like you are tied to a pole or something. Understand other people's position first because how else will they know that you are on the same page with them?

The woman in the example above told the attendant her preferences, but the attendant ignored them. She thought pressing forward was going to change her mind and that, eventually, the woman would be happy and grateful to her for having tried to change her mind and finally succeeded. The buyer was a completely different person with a completely different background and, of course, a completely different way of life and values.

What mattered to the attendant did not matter to the buyer and that's where the attendant got it all wrong. She felt her habit was the best and that people should always strive to be like her. It's wrong because the more you try to impose your habit on someone, the farther you push them from changing their already formed decision.

3. What does it do for you even if they give in? You reel out your behavior pattern to your friends and perhaps on your 500th attempt they decide to give it a shot. What have you gained? Imagine being surrounded by people who acted and behaved like you simply because you have succeeded in convincing them that their own version of unique and existence is not good enough. Imagine a world filled with everyone acting like you.

    How boring and lacking in spontaneity will that be. Of course, when the people around you get finally convinced to do what you want them to do, it comes at a big cost to your relationship with them.

    Making people want to accept you for who they are means to the point of wanting to change who they are and what they stand for is never a solid foundation to build anything upon. Other people shouldn't need to adapt your own version, and understanding this means that you respect and appreciate everyone for who or what they are. This is enough.

The main question then is, why should people have to act in a kind of way for you to feel satisfied? If that lady ended up buying those books in the example above, what would the lady have derived from it? A moment of satisfaction at being right?

Finally, it's way better to listen to people's wants and desires and help them achieve it than to impose your own desires on them. If you want to change their decision, then you need to prove that you understand them and why they really want something the way it is.

Chapter 12: What Are Mini Habits and Why Are They Important?

Take a moment and imagine what it would look like taking only little steps at getting yourself better and then in the process making impactful changes and meaningful changes to your life. If this is the first time you are hearing of mini-habits then you have just enough to learn here.

The word mini-habits is just what it sounds like. It gives us the idea that we can actually do numerous little things and watch it add up to great things. As I'm sure you've heard it said countless times, the little things in life are what really matter.

Do them consistently and religiously, and you will find that your life is way better and those around you will be happier.

Imagine reading about happenings around the world every day. Imagine how well informed and versed you would have become by the end of, say, a month or even a year. You would have accumulated more knowledge about things happening around you and will be more likely to partake in discussions about recent happenings. In short, you would have become a more interesting person.

This is not the only thing that your mini-habits do for you though. They go a long way to impact your body and mind and, in the long run, affect how quickly and permanently you can switch old harmful habits for new and beneficial ones.

Now, let's look at the benefits of mini-habits.

1. You create an atmosphere of success: When we set very large goals, we look to ourselves as being incapable of achieving these goals and we look to the goals as being impossible. What mini-habits do for us is that they make it easier for us to reach our goals. When you set small targets, it's usually easier to meet them and also to accomplish them within a very short period as compared to when you decide to take on your task fully without first breaking them down into smaller, achievable bits.

    Take for example, instead of piling up your unanswered calls and telling yourself that you will return all calls eventually, why not return the last call immediately or after some reasonable time than allowing it to pile up. Better still, you could fix a time for when you want to return your call and stick to it if you are so busy when the call came in. If the task were bigger, such as writing an article or writing an essay for a competition, then you could fix a time limit for every task. Divide your work into smaller parts and make them look simple enough to achieve.

A fixed time limit for research; another fixed time for giving an introduction; another fixed time for writing the body of the essay or article and so on and so forth. With this, you quickly find yourself completing your Herculean task in no time. When you do these, it takes away the feeling of failure which comes from having procrastinated what you ought to do and also the feeling of failure for not doing enough.

Another thing about these small tasks is that you get to start with the mindset of succeeding because you have your activities all planned out before you and it seems quite easy for you. Starting off with the mindset of succeeding could help you eventually succeed.

2. Mini-habits help you change how you view your capabilities: When you accomplish the small things, then you start to believe that you can actually do better than this or better than you did your last time. You boost your confidence, and it gives you a better understanding of what you are better at and also gives you a positive sense of your abilities.

3. You find motivation: While it is very easy to come by motivation (almost everyone is a willing motivational speaker), it is very difficult to make use of that surge of power you get at that moment you get motivated. If it, in fact, comes by, it gets used up very quickly and then you are back to square one, doubting yourself and all the motivational speaker said. This is why mini-habits are very important.

Your mini-habits do not rely on your motivation to get things done, it relies on your willpower. As you move on you begin to feel the joy of having started and almost reaching completion, you can then find the motivation to finish what you started.

With mini-habits, you create a series of changes that you have always wanted to accomplish all along. It helps to build your ability to start bigger things and actually finish them. It's like wanting to stay fit, and you start with push-ups every day and stay true to the daily exercise.

With time, you add more exercises to your routine, and just like that, you have developed a new habit that keeps you healthy and fit.

To summarize, this how mini-habits work. First, you pick a huge task you would like to do and pick a date you would want it finished. The next thing is to shrink these habits until they are very small. If you want to write an article, then start with 50 words every day. Do you want to know more about the happenings around you? Then read the news every day. Do you want to be fit? Start every day with a push-up.

Looks easy, right? It's actually very easy. It works, and it will be easy because our brains are wired to fall for the smaller things that do not require too much at a time. You see fifty-word poems and you jump at it. You can do that because you have built yourself to write every day. Let's go through ten daily mini-habits you should keep up with to become a better person.

Compliment one person, daily. Your compliment should, however, be genuine. No one is asking you to fake your real feelings just in the name of developing a new habit. You might as well be living a lie in your habit at the end of the day. Think two positive thoughts every day. Meditate for one minute. Name three things you're thankful for, daily. Write fifty words. Read. Do one push-up. Drink one glass of water. Go outside. And take 100 steps.

You can change basically any area of your life. It takes just one mini-habit at a time and then you are better off this month than you were the last month. Remove the pressure and expectations and simply allow yourself to start.

Conclusion

Regardless of how fundamental it is to keep good long-term habits and actually strengthen them, it is also quite important to note that there is something called mini-habits, without which our long term habits will not come to fulfillment.

As important as forming positive habits are, they are *your* positive habits. Please, do not impose them on anyone. We can grow continuously; attaining one habit does not prevent you from starting another. Also, the detractors become heavier when you are at the earliest stage. At the point when you are feeling anxious and are pressured to give up, it will be important to create the right atmosphere that you want. For this, you should work to enhance your willpower. This way, you become more willing to go through it all and grow.

After these stages, you are less likely to fall prey to any other distraction on your journey to success. By then, they must have become a part of your character.

References

Kiderra, I. (2016, May 26). How the brain make – and breaks – a habit. Retrieved from https://ucsdnews.ucsd.edu/pressrelease/how_the_brain_makes_and_breaks _a_habit

Oshin, M. (n.d.). How clutter causes stress and anxiety (and what you can do about it). Retrieved from https://mayooshin.com/clutter-causes-stress-anxiety/

Tañedo, E. (2019, July 2). 5 ways decluttering can improve your daily life. Retrieved from https://management30.com/blog/5-ways-decluttering-can-improve-your-daily-life/

The ridiculously thorough guide to decluttering your home. (n.d.). Retrieved from https://www.budgetdumpster.com/resources/how-to-declutter-your-home.php

Williams, R. (2018, June 18). 5 decluttering tips to enhance addiction recovery and maintain new healthy habits. Retrieved from https://www.newharbinger.com/blog/5-decluttering-tips-enhance-addiction-recovery-and-maintain-new-healthy-habits

Made in the USA
Columbia, SC
11 May 2020